POCKET BOWIE WISDOM

INSPIRATIONAL WORDS FROM A ROCK LEGEND

POCKET BOWIE WISDOM

INSPIRATIONAL WORDS FROM A ROCK LEGEND

hardie grant books

CONTENTS

DAVID BOWIE ON...
MUSIC

'I needed to sing
because nobody else was
singing my songs.'

Fresh Air, NPR, 4th September 2002

'I suppose for me as an artist
it wasn't always just about
expressing my work; I really
wanted, more than anything
else, to contribute in some way
to the culture I was living in.'

GQ, 17th October 2002

'I'm just an individual who doesn't feel that I need to have somebody qualify my work in any particular way. I'm working for me.'

60 Minutes, CBS News, 28th July 2002

'A lot of what I've done is about alienation... about where you fit in society.'

Orlando Sentinel, 18th September 1987

'All my big mistakes are when I try to second-guess or please an audience. My work is always stronger when I get very selfish about it.'

'To not be modest about it, you'll find that with only a couple of exceptions, most of the musicians that I've worked with have done their best work by far with me.'

Livewire, 16th June 2002

'I certainly don't understand half the stuff I write. I can look back on a song I've just written and it means something entirely different now because of my new circumstances.'

NME, 22nd July 1972

'My performances have got
to be theatrical experiences
for me as well as for the
audience. I don't want to climb
out of my fantasies in order
to go up onstage – I want to
take them on stage with me.'

Rolling Stone, 1st April 1971

MUSIC

'I guess any list of advice
I have to offer to a musician
always ends with, "If it itches,
go and see a doctor."'

Berklee Commencement Address, 8th May 1999

'You know, what I do
is not terribly intellectual.
I'm a pop singer for
Christ's sake.'

GQ, 17th October 2002

'[Music has] been both
my doorway of perception
and the house that I live in.'

'It wasn't so much about how I felt about things, but rather, how things around me felt. To put it simply, I had discovered the Englishman's true place in rock and roll.'

Berklee Commencement Address, 8th May 1999

'What I do is I write
mainly about very personal
and rather lonely feelings,
and I explore them in
a different way each time.'

GQ, 17th October 2002

'We were terribly excited,
and I think we took
it on our shoulders that
we were creating the
21st century in 1971.'

Fresh Air, NPR, 4th September 2002

'I had to resign myself, many years ago, that I'm not too articulate when it comes to explaining how I feel about things. But my music does it for me, it really does. There, in the chords and melodies, is everything I want to say.'

Livewire, 16th June 2002

DAVID BOWIE ON...

FAME

FAME

'I'm an instant star.
Just add water and stir.'

Valentines & Vitriol by Rex Reed, Delacorte Press, 1977

'I want to know why
[the media] wasted all that
time and effort and paper
on my clothes and my pose.
Why? Because I was
a dangerous statement.'

Playboy, September 1976

'I knew I was good, I knew
I could write. I also knew you
could get laid really easily.'

Complex, August 2003

'I'm going to be huge,
and it's quite frightening
in a way. Because I know
that when I reach my peak
and it's time for me
to be brought down it will
be with a bump.'

Melody Maker, 22nd January 1972

FAME

'I definitely like being a star. It's the only thing that I can do that doesn't bore me.'

Melody Maker, 22nd January 1972

'I think fame itself is not
a rewarding thing. The most
you can say is that it gets
you a seat in restaurants.'

Q Magazine, April 1990

DAVID BOWIE ON...

IDENTITY

'I mean, my whole life is made up of experimentation, curiosity and anything that seemed at all appealing.'

Time Out, April 1983

'I've always felt bemused
at being called the chameleon
of rock. Doesn't a chameleon
exert tremendous energy
to become indistinguishable
from its environment?'

Esquire, March 2004

IDENTITY

'Aspects of your own life get mixed into the image that you're trying to project as a character, so it becomes a hybrid of reality and fantasy. And that is an extraordinary situation.'

Telegraph, 14th December 1996

**'I am only the person
the greatest number
of people believe I am.'**

Q Magazine, October 1999

'I pieced together bits
and pieces of other artists and
they all became this rather
grand, stylish lad, Ziggy.'

BBC Radio 1, 8th January 1997

IDENTITY

'It's all artifice.'

Fresh Air, NPR, 4th September 2002

DAVID BOWIE ON...

HIMSELF

'I'm just a cosmic yob, I suppose.'

Melody Maker, 22nd January 1972

'What I have is a malevolent curiosity. That's what drives my need to write and what probably leads me to look at things a little askew.'

New York Daily News, 9th June 2002

'I change every day.
I'm not outrageous.
I'm David Bowie.'

Melody Maker, 22nd January 1972

'People are much more
important to me than ideas.'

Jackie, 10th May 1970

'I seem to draw a lot of
fantasies out of people.'

Russell Harty Show, 20th January 1973

'I'm always amazed that people take what I say seriously. I don't even take what I *am* seriously.'

**'If there's one thing
I've contributed, it's a great
dollop of uncertainty.
For better or worse.'**

NME, 13th September 1980

'I'm quite certain I wouldn't
have survived the Seventies
if I'd carried on doing
what I was doing.'

Telegraph, 14th December 1996

'At least I wear a pair
of women's high heels when
I meet our Prime Minister!'

Newsnight, 1999

'If it's wearing a pink hat
and a red nose, and it plays
a guitar upside down, I will
go and look at it. I love to see
people being dangerous.'

Rolling Stone, April 1999

'I already consider myself responsible for a whole new school of pretension.'

Rolling Stone, 12th February 1976

'It's not infrequent that I wake up on a chilly morning and wish I was in Kyoto or somewhere and in a Zen monastery.'

NME, 13th September 1980

'I think there's still room for adventure. One of us is going to stumble on it sooner or later … please, God, let it be me!'

Q Magazine, April 1990

DAVID BOWIE ON...

LOVE

LOVE

'The reason you don't want to make a commitment is not that you're such a freewheeling, adventurous person, it's because you're scared shitless that it will turn out like your mother and father.'

Interview Magazine, May 1990

LOVE

**'I'm frighteningly happy.
I don't see ever wanting
to change things in
my personal life.'**

New York Daily News, 9th June 2002

'[My ex-wife] and I knew each other because we were both going out with the same man.'

'Marrying my wife.
That's the most successful
thing I ever did in my life.
Nothing else counts.'

Interview with Simon Witter, 4th October 1995

LOVE

'I stumbled onto bliss.
And I have no intention
of finding my way back out.'

New York Daily News, 9th June 2002

'The differences between you will be the key to love... These are the things to be treasured above all else. The similarities will take care of themselves.'

LOVE

[On the secret to great relationships:]
'Complete and absolute generosity with the duvet.'

DAVID BOWIE ON...
LIFE

'I love humanity,
I adore it,
it's sensational,
sensuous, exciting.'

Interview Magazine, March 1973

'The problems begin when
you try to intellectualise.
Especially when you've just
done a gram of cocaine.'

NME, 16th April 1983

'I've come to the realisation that I have absolutely no idea what I'm doing half the time.'

NME, 29th September 1984

'The truth is of course is
that there is no journey.
We are arriving and departing
all at the same time.'

Livewire, 16th June 2002

'I thrive on mistakes.
If I haven't made three good
mistakes in a week, then
I'm not worth anything.
You only learn from mistakes.'

NME, 12th November 1977

'I really had a hunger to experience everything that life had to offer, from the opium den to whatever… Anything that Western culture has to offer – I've put myself through most of it.'

Telegraph, 14th December 1996

'Once you lose that sense
of wonder at being alive,
you're pretty much
on the way out.'

Everyone Loves You When You're Dead by Neil Strauss, Canongate Books, 2011

'As you get older the questions come down to about two or three. How long? And what do I do with the time I've got left?'

New York Times, 9th June 2002

'I don't think I ever felt
that life was very long.
It was certainly no surprise
to me that I got old.'

Telegraph, 14th December 1996

'Make the best of every moment. We're not evolving. We're not going anywhere.'

Esquire, March 2004

'I've always thought the only thing to do was to try to go through life as Superman, right from the word go. I felt far too insignificant as just another person.'

Playboy, September 1976

'I don't know where
I'm going from here,
but I promise it won't
be boring.'

Onstage at his 50th birthday party, reported by *CNN*, 29th September 1998

Pocket Bowie Wisdom

First published in 2016 by Hardie Grant Books, an imprint of Hardie Grant Publishing

Hardie Grant Books (UK)
5th & 6th Floors
52–54 Southwark Street
London SE1 1UN

Hardie Grant Books (Australia)
Ground Floor, Building 1
658 Church Street
Melbourne, VIC 3121

hardiegrantbooks.com

British Library Cataloguing-in-Publication Data. A catalogue record for this book is available from the British Library.

UK ISBN: 978-1-78488-072-9
US ISBN: 978-1-78488-073-6

Publisher: Kate Pollard
Senior Editor: Kajal Mistry
Editorial Assistant: Hannah Roberts
Art Direction: Claire Warner Studio
Cover Illustration © Kayci Wheatley, www.kayciwheatley.com
Image on page 27 © Mike Zuidgeest (NL); Image on page 79 © Martin Vanco (SK)
Colour Reproduction by p2d

Printed and bound in China by Toppan Leefung, DongGuan City, China